Persuasion Secrets of the World's Most Charismatic & Influential Villains

By Ben Settle
©2016-2018

*"You were right about me all along, Mr. Kent.
I am the villain of the story."*
— Lex Luthor
Smallville

ISBN-13: 978-1535359955
ISBN-10: 1535359951

iv

Table of Contents

Legal Notices Even Villains Dare Not Ignore!

by mail at PO Box 1056, Gold Beach, OR 97444.

For more information, please read the "Disclosures and Disclaimers" section at the end of this book.

Published by Settle, LLC (the "Publisher") with the help of MakeRight Publishing, Inc.

Acknowledgments

The content in this book was originally written for a site called *The Proper Villains*. The site was brilliant in its use of infotainment and the "villain" theme to teach vital self-improvement life lessons for men. (Ranging from how to attract women, to investing, to firearms, and everything in between.)

Anyway, my villain alter ego was "Rood" — and I wrote mostly about success, mindset, persuasion, and business-related topics. The most important thing I wrote was a 10-part series on how to become a charismatic and influential Villain. Everything you need to know to be attractive, persuasive, respected, wealthy, and even admired by others was in those articles.

Unfortunately, the site has mysteriously vanished. At the time of this writing, all the articles, content, and lessons were wiped clean from thc Internet. You cannot find them archived or cached anywhere. And, I have no idea if the site will ever return.

Fortunately, I saved my articles and am reprinting the 10-part series (with slight modifications) here in this short, easy-to-read book. This content has made a dramatic difference in my life. And, I believe it can do the same for you, too.

Enjoy…

Ben Settle

AKA "Rood"

Who is Rood?

The authorities are aware of Rood's Villainous ambitions. And it amuses him how they can do nothing to stop him, because he masterfully uses a "loophole" in the law that says it's not illegal to plan to take over the world, since no crime has (yet) been committed.

Rood is an entrepreneur, author, and self-described "Anti-professional." He is also a master of influence and persuasion, and spends all his time in his lair writing books, newsletters, and twisted monster novels to finance his world domination plans.

Rood makes no attempt to hide his real identity, his business dealings, or his mission to force the world to submit to his authority. He openly mocks his hero enemies, and the planet's leaders, military, and police are terrified of the coming day when he decides to make his move...

Introduction
-
The Most Influential Guy in the Room

"Well, John wasn't exactly the boogeyman. He was the one you sent to kill the fucking boogeyman!"

— Viggo Tarasov
John Wick

Several years ago, I was introduced to an unusually persuasive Villain through business.

There was nothing "special" about him at a glance. In fact, he had below average looks (balding, short, a bit of a gut). He was no more intelligent or better dressed than any other person you'd meet on the street (if anything, he dressed kind of goofy and said he barely graduated high school). And, he wasn't handed any advantages by birthright (he grew up in a lower middle class home).

In many ways, he seemed like the epitome of common.

Yet, he was one of the most uncommon men I ever met.

By that I mean, things just fell into place for him.

Everyone respected him (even his enemies). Colleagues and business partners eagerly submitted to him. Beautiful women went out of their way just to be around him. And, people practically stood in line to talk to him, befriend him, and help him if he asked for it.

He was truly a powerful man.

And, he had everything a guy could want:

- Money
- Fame
- Power
- Respect

- Influence
- Adventures
- Dames
- Opportunity
- Privilege
- Submission
- Access
- Even knowledge denied other men

Now, you may be wondering... what was this otherwise "average" man's secret to obtaining such power and influence? And (even more importantly) how can YOU achieve the same?

The answer: *Charisma.*

The definition of charisma is:

1. Compelling attractiveness or charm that can inspire devotion in others.

2. (pl. charismata |-ˌmətə|) (also charism |ˈkarˌizəm|) a divinely conferred power or talent.

If there's one attribute that differentiates a true Villain from the masses of schlubs and wannabes it's charisma.

If you have charisma the world will hand you (on a solid gold platter) anything you want. In fact, once you gain this mysterious power denied the vast majority of ordinary men, you will find things mysteriously fall into place for you, too. Job promotions are handed to you with little or no effort. Dames you want pursue you, instead of you pursuing them. Money problems vanish seemingly overnight. Customers in business buy from you without hesitation. People in your social life are eager to become your minions and henchmen, to be used at your disposal. Persuading others to do your bidding becomes as routine and effortless as ordering a burger. And conquering the world becomes a tangible, attainable goal.

All of which begs the question:

How can you become charismatic?

Below are ten secrets of extraordinarily charismatic Villains. Each has been wielded — like a weapon of mass influence — by the greatest Villains in history. And, by making them a part of your everyday life you can start enjoying the fruits of being a charismatic Villain, too — with the world as your oyster — in weeks and months, instead of years and decades.

Here they are:

1. Bow only at the altar of your mission
2. Nix all neediness
3. Pay yourself first
4. Keep a "screw you" fund
5. Shove people off their pedestals
6. Slay your inner nice guy
7. Stake the time vampires
8. Ignore the sheep
9. Submit to patience
10. Be the Joker

The rest of this book will go into depth on each of these. When you are ready to begin simply turn the page...

Chapter 1

-

A Villain Without a Mission Is Like a Man Without Testicles

"Tony, this is your Ninth Symphony. What a masterpiece. Look at that. This is your legacy."

— Obadiah Stane
(AKA, the villain "Iron Monger")
Ironman

Back in the early days of my business career I knew the most socially awkward man you could ever imagine.

For example:

He was needy and clingy with everyone. He was depressing to talk to and a vicious, passive-aggressive gossiper. He would sweat, turn red, and go "mute" just being in a girl's presence. He looked like his mom still dressed him. Guys openly mocked him, he had zero friends, and, worst of all, his personality was so repugnant... he couldn't keep a job for more than a few months before he was fired.

He Was a Pitiful Wretch of a Man

And, he was so pathetic you couldn't even feel sorry for him.

Whenever a guy shoved him out of the way or girls insulted him to his face, you understood. He all but asked to be treated that way.

It was painful just watching this guy interact with people. And, if anyone looked like the poster child for failure, it was him.

Now, fast forward ten years later.

Today this man is a multi-millionaire, high paid speaker, published author, and philanthropist. People practically fight each other just to have the chance to do business with him. He always has a beautiful dame on his arm. He drives $100,000 sport cars. And, he lives the kind of lifestyle 99.9% of men will never know.

A successful Villain thru and thru.

But, how did he do it?

How did he go from super schlub to super Villain?

What was his secret?

Answer:

The Guy Decided to Pursue a Mission

A mission (in his case, build a multi-million-dollar business and never have to be under anyone else's authority) that transcended himself. He started out near penniless, poured his heart and soul into it every day, and went after it without apology, pause, or apprehension.

The result was a total transformation in his life — financially, emotionally, and professionally.

That's the kind of transformation a man with a mission can experience.

In fact, when you encounter a Villain with a clearly defined mission you will instantly know it.

You'll see it in his eyes.

You'll hear it in his voice (especially when he tells "war stories" about pursuing his mission).

And, you'll feel it in the vibe he gives off just being in his presence.

There is something about a Villain with a mission other people are irresistibly drawn to. A Villain on a mission doesn't care about what anyone — man or woman — thinks about him. Instead, he cares only for his mission. As a result, women can't help but be attracted to him (regardless of his looks), and will even compete with each other to be his minion. Men, on the other hand, are inspired and intimidated by him. They want to be like him (even if they think they can never be him), eagerly submit to him, and stand in line just to become one of his lowly henchmen.

A mission gives a Villain charisma.

Charisma gives a Villain power and influence.

And power and influence gives a Villain the world.

But, It All *Starts* with Your Mission

A Villain without a mission is as useful as a eunuch. Just as a man without testicles cannot procreate, has no drive, and is pitied by men and women alike, a Villain without a mission has no value to those he wishes to subjugate. People will, in fact, reject, mock, and be repelled by a Villain without a mission.

If you don't have a mission, you must get one.

Today.

No excuses or putting it off until the New Year or when you're "ready."

What kind of mission should you pursue?

That is entirely your choice and nobody can make it for you.

It can be financial (building a business empire), or creative (becoming a world-famous musician, best-selling author, or celebrity actor), or religious (founding a church or organization to support your faith), or becoming the best there is in the world at a particular skill (shooting, poker, hunting, racing, professional sports, etc.), or anything you want.

A mission is a personal quest and I can't tell you what yours should be.

What I can tell you is, once you do have a mission you must nurture, protect, and ruthlessly pursue it. It must be the first thing you work on when you wake up in the morning, and the last thing on your mind when you drift off to sleep. Friends, dames, even family must come second, with your mission being your most urgent priority. I am not saying to shirk any familial or marital responsibilities. But realize your loved ones' happiness, security, and emotional/financial well-being trickle down from you — the man on a mission in their lives. It's like when flying a major airline. If the cabin loses pressure an oxygen mask drops down and you are told to put it on before trying to assist anyone around you. So it is for a man with a mission. Your mission is your oxygen mask.

Bow only to the altar of your mission.

Not to dames.

Not to friends.

And not to another person's company, government, or society.

Put your mission first and you will automatically become a charismatic and influential Villain. Just the decision to achieve a mission — and then working towards it each day — will set forces in motion that will change your life, and the lives of those you love and wish to rule over.

In time, money will be attracted to you.

Dames will flock to you.

Family, friends, and acquaintances will respect you.

And power, influence, opportunity, access, and the best of life's pleasures will be yours for the taking.

Yes, you will have setbacks.

Yes, you will have challenges.

And yes, you will want to quit at times — and probably have to hear the opinions of lesser men who are afraid of your success and the power it will grant you. After all, in nature if you put crabs in a bucket, and one tries to climb out, the other crabs will pull it back in. Such is the fate of any man who decides to pursue a mission.

So be ready for challenges, and don't be surprised when they happen. Just realize the thrill of achieving your mission and the joy of working on it will give you the greatest satisfaction you can ever experience. A bad day working on your mission is better than a good day living a boring life of mediocrity like everyone else you know.

And the best part is, all it takes is a decision to define your mission and go after it. The rest will take care of itself.

Chapter 2
-
Annihilate Your Neediness

*"Do you *feel* in charge?"*

— Bane
The Dark Knight Rises

Recently, my fellow Villain Greg Perry sent me an email illustrating the #1 thing that'll kill your charisma, confidence, attraction, influence... and other attributes a Villain must have in order to conquer and rule.

Here is What Happened:

Like me, Greg lives a private life in his Villain's lair.

Like me, he can only handle people in small doses.

And, like me, he has a low tolerance for people who don't value his time.

Anyway, he was telling me about how he'd been getting phone calls from friends needing to "have lunch" or "come visit" or asking him "WHY do I never get time with you?"... and so on. And, it got him to thinking about why he never goes out of his way to visit them or grant them his valuable time and attention.

Yes, he loves his friends and family.

Yes, he respects them.

And yes, he would do anything for them.

But, he doesn't go out of his way to talk to them, hang out with them, or visit them. If anything, he thinks of excuses not to want to be around them.

Now, contrast that to my friendship with Greg.

We have known each other for almost 15 years. We have never once met in person. And, we have only spoken by phone a few times, and primarily communicate by email.

Yet, here is what he said:

> *"I like all these friends, a lot, but really, the only one I really would ON MY OWN make any effort to see if we lived closer is ROOD. I just don't have enough in common with ALL THESE MEN to make an effort any more. Strange since you and I have never talked in person isn't it? But I consider you TOPS on my friend list, and even then you're light years ahead of whoever is #2."*

Why would Greg have this attitude?

Why does he hold me in so much more esteem and respect than he does people he lives closer to, has known longer, and has broken bread with?

And, why do I have the exact same opinion of him?

In a word:

Neediness.

Guys like Greg and I have zero neediness. And because of that, people in our lives want to be around us, listen to us, and get nervous when we don't grant them attention. As a result, it's very easy for us to recruit henchmen and minions. If we want social interaction, we get it on a dime (without begging, shaming, or complaining). And, when we require a favor or request, they are granted without hesitation or drama.

Hear ye me and pay attention.

There are few things better you can do to:

1. Be more charismatic...

2. Improve your relationships (romantic, business partnerships, friendships, professional, family, etc.) and...

3. Attract people and opportunity into your life...

... than by simply *not* being needy.

Being needy means you need someone or something — whether it be a woman, a job, a favor, someone's attention, a population's vote, or anything else you want. Neediness repels people away from you. They can sense it in your words, your tonalities, and your body language.

Nobody wants to be around a needy man.

(Do you?)

Neediness kills everything about you that is attractive, charismatic, and influential. Frankly, a needy man cannot, by definition, be a Villain, no matter how many other Villain attributes he has.

Below are a few neediness "tells."

Ask yourself if you're guilty of doing any of these things:

- Talk a lot when trying to persuade someone to do what you want. (An idea, a plan, a heist, or even getting a date with a dame.)

- Asking people to spend time with you, instead of inviting them to.

- Constantly checking your phone when waiting for a reply. (Whether it be a dame, tonight's plans with friends, someone you're selling a house to, anything.)

- Afraid of not being liked.

- Complain about people not making time for you.

- Get emotional when someone tells you "no."

- Always available, no matter what.

- Fear losing people in your life.

- Show respect to people who don't respect you back.

- Work on other peoples' missions before working on your own each day. (Including going to work in the morning before putting time in on your mission first.)

- Have trouble saying "no" to people.

- Apologize all the time.
- And the list goes on...

If you are guilty of doing any of the above then you are a needy man. And, a needy man can never be a true Villain.

That's the bad news.

The good news?

It's simple to stop your needy ways, even if you've been needy your entire life. Whenever you learn something new (like how to not be needy) you go through these stages:

- **Unconscious incompetence** (i.e. you don't know you're needy)

- **Conscious incompetence** (i.e. you're aware you're needy but don't know how to fix it)

- **Conscious competence** (i.e. you're not needy when you consciously remind yourself about it)

- **Unconscious competence** (i.e. you automatically never act needy, without reminding yourself)

Before reading this chapter you were in stage 1.

As you were reading until now, you were in stage 2.

For now on, you'll be in stage 3 until, one day, you don't have to think about it and are stage 4. The key to getting to this level fast is to always be vigilant and constantly remind yourself not to do the needy things listed above (or any other needy behaviors not listed).

What's the single best way to get started?

Simply (Starting *Today*) Withhold Interest from People

In other words:

Put yourself and your goals, interests, and desires before anyone else's. Don't ask people to hang out with you anymore. Instead, invite them to join you somewhere you're *already* going to be whether they show or not. (And not caring if they come either way — easiest way ever to prevent people from flaking out on you, too.) Disappear from your social circle for a while to focus on your mission. And, position yourself as the person at the top of the mountain — who's hard to get to and perceived as more valuable than the schlub at the bottom of the mountain who's always available and easy to access.

Maybe this sounds counterintuitive.

Perhaps even a bit jerkish.

You best get used to it if you're going to be a Villain. When you become a Villain you're no longer in the same soulless democracy/popularity contest as your friends, family, and colleagues.

A Villain's Life is Not a Democracy — It's a Dictatorship

And you're the dictator.

Ever see a needy dictator before?

Me either.

And by simply eliminating neediness you will instantly elevate your value to the world. You will automatically be more charismatic to dames, would-be henchmen, and those you wish to rule. Plus, you will begin to experience a peace of mind and confidence you didn't even know existed.

One last thing:

Don't beat yourself up if you've been acting needy.

Even the best of men fall into neediness at times. For many years it was the biggest mistake I made, and it chased away more opportunities (and people) than I care to admit. I would do everything else right, but this one thing — being needy — sabotaged my progress.

The key is to catch yourself so you don't do it anymore.

And, if you do, learn from the mistake and move forward.

In the next chapter I'll show you how to give yourself some "insurance" from being needy — especially when it comes to finances. (So you don't "need" a job or client you hate or ever have to go into debt or borrow money from someone.)

Chapter 3

-

Selfishly Pay Yourself First

"Yes. We can rebuild. Enlarge the containment field. Make it bigger and stronger than ever! But we need money."

— Doctor Octopus
Spiderman 2

Back in 1926, George Clason published his book ***The Richest Man in Babylon***. The book is mostly about a poor man asking a rich man about how he got wealthy. It's also considered a "must read" by top financial authors, and its timeless advice has created fortunes for thousands of men over the past several decades.

The book's first (and most important) financial rule?

"Ten percent of everything you earn is yours to keep."

i.e., Pay yourself first.

That means the first 10% (minimum) of your paycheck belongs to you.

Not the electric bill.

Or the IRS.

Or debt collectors.

Or loan sharks.

Or anyone else.

Instead, the first 10% (more is better) is yours to save and invest with, so it can bring you back many more dollars without you having to manually labor for it. I'm not saying to not pay your taxes, debts, or bills. I'm simply saying to become financially independent you must pay yourself first — without excuse, apology, or exception.

And make no mistake about it:

Financial independence is mandatory if you wish to be a charismatic and influential Villain who commands respect, attracts the best minions and sidekicks, and has the money to finance your heists, schemes, plans, and Mission.

After all, how can you attain world conquest if you're always worried about money?

And it all begins with paying yourself first.

Making this one (simple) change in your finances instantly puts you on the road to financial independence. It gives you a mental and emotional toughness lacking in 90% of men today. It forces you to cut out the fat in your finances (like daily overpriced sugar coffees, weekend bar-hopping, dining out, wasting money on useless crap just to impress others, etc.) And, you'll automatically develop the creativity a Villain needs for making money when your plans go all to hell and you need cash flow quick.

More:

There's another (even more crucial) way of paying yourself first you will probably never hear from another book, class, or financial expert.

Here's what I mean:

Several years ago, like most men, I woke up each day, went to a job, and gave that company the best and most productive part of my day... only to come home too exhausted to work on my own Mission. Later, when I became a freelance copywriter, I spent all my time (including the first part of my day — when I was at my best and most focused) making my clients rich while I barely scraped by. Then one day, I got fed up with spinning my wheels and gave myself one year to liberate myself from needing clients — where I could sell my own products and keep all the money instead of selling everyone else's products and keeping only a fraction of what I earned for them. (My ads earned clients millions of dollars, while I barely met my bills.)

The first thing I did?

I decided the first hour of every day belonged to me.

To work on my own projects.

To create my own products.

And to write ads to sell my own books, newsletters, and novels.

It didn't matter how busy I was. It didn't matter if I had multiple impossible deadlines. It didn't matter if a client insisted I drop everything on a dime with the looming threat of being firing if I didn't comply. No matter what happened, how busy I got, or how many threats came... the first hour of each day was mine.

The result?

Within six months (half the time I planned for) I reached my goal and have been devoting all my working time towards my Mission and nobody else's since.

And you can do the same thing.

Starting today pay yourself the first 10% of every dollar you earn, and invest the first hour of every day into your Mission.

It'll be rough at first trying to adapt.

But you just have to sac up and ride it out.

Soon, you won't even miss that 10% of your paycheck or that first hour of the day. In fact, you'll start whacking away at debt and notice your income going up. Same with your time. By keeping that first hour for yourself, you'll have more (not less) free time for your Mission as your schedule adapts and you become more productive.

Bottom line?

Pay yourself first — both financially and in time.

Doing so makes you the master of time and money, instead of a slave to time and money.

Now, turn the page to find out the first thing to do with the 10% you're keeping so you never have to rely on anyone else for money, a job, or a loan ever again.

Chapter 4
-
Secure Your "Screw You" Fund

"I have 3 million dollars in a suitcase...
that long term enough for ya?"

— Hit-Girl
Kickass

The above quote is from one of the world's top direct response copywriters. He's a man who has been homeless, broke, and scrounging for change in his couch cushions just to eat... to being not only filthy rich, but one of the great marketing minds of our time.

He also regularly dispenses a powerful piece of advice about money every Villain should read, memorize, and implement immediately.

Here Is the Story:

In his magnificent guide, *Kick Ass Copywriting Secrets of a Marketing Rebel,* John talks about how, many years ago, he had a long dry spell in his business where he couldn't find any clients. At the time, he was regularly charging $15,000 to write a single sales letter. But things had become so dire financially he took a client for just $2,000.

That's how desperate he had become.

And, he really needed the cash.

But what happened was, the client screwed around with his pay. He was supposed to send John half the fee up front. Instead, he only paid part of the fee with a note saying something about leaving more of the "carrot" out so John would work harder for it. (I am going on memory, but that is the gist of it.)

Naturally, that pissed John off.

And, despite his needing the dough he told the client to hit the bricks.

He wasn't going to work with a guy like that.

And, he went on his merry way.

Anyway, here is why I tell this story:

This was one of many incidents that prompted John to start what he called a "screw you" fund — which every Villain should have. In fact, just possessing this fund will grant you a powerful kind of charisma and confidence you cannot fake.

But, what is a "screw you" fund, exactly?

The answer is simple:

It's six months to a year of income set aside that, if you never touch it, it's done its job. John recommends you never put it in anything riskier than a bank CD. But I believe it should be kept in <u>cash</u> — and well hidden. (Preferably not on your property so it can't be seized in a raid, stolen by thieves, or pocketed by a treacherous henchman or spurned dame.)

How does having a screw you fund make you more charismatic and influential?

It goes back to neediness.

When you don't need someone's money, paycheck, fee, job, business deal, etc you will grant yourself a power few men will ever experience. When you have a year's worth of money stashed away you have no problem turning down bad opportunities. You can pass up heists that haven't been well planned. You can tell the overweight schlub boss or client where to stick it if he disrespects you. If you ever get pinched, audited, or shaken down by a crooked cop you have bail, lawyer, or (if necessary) leave-the-country-tonight cash ready to access.

Another quote from John Carlton comes to mind:

> *"Having money will solve a lot of problems not having money creates."*

It's true.

And, it's especially true for a Villain.

So start your screw you fund today.

I suggest you fund it with the percentage of your income you're now paying yourself first, selling off any possessions you don't need, and even taking a night job to create this fund as fast as possible.

After that the magic happens.

People will instantly notice a bold new confidence in you. They'll hear it in your voice. See it in your body language. And smell it in your attitude.

They will know, without you saying a word, you don't need their money.

You don't need their job.

And you sure as hell don't need them.

Chapter 5

-

Ruthlessly Knock People Off Their Pedestals

"I was thinking that you're the most exquisite creature I've ever seen. And this [glass] needs ice."

— Sebastian Shaw
X-Men: First Class

Let me tell you another story.

Recently, one of my friends got dumped by his dame and was having a tough time dealing with it. He's already financially successful and commands the respect of his employees, colleagues, and peers. But, his dame gave him the slip and it drove him crazy thinking about how it happened. After all, this man has money, power, and admiration, what else could his dame want?

My diagnosis?

He put her on a pedestal.

He damn near worshipped her.

And that, in my humble (but accurate) opinion, was his downfall. So I told him henceforth to never, ever, Ever, *Ever,* *EVER* put a dame on a pedestal. I don't care if it's someone he's dating. Or a girlfriend. Or, even a wife.

First of all, it makes her think you're weak (whether she admits it or realizes it or not).

And secondly, there are practical reasons for this.

Like your peace of mind.

Your dignity.

And, being perceived by other people (not just dames) as a strong leader to be followed and submitted to... not a pathetic schlub to be pitied and barked orders at. Can you imagine any of Lex Luthor's henchmen, minions, dames, underlings, or employees (including the police on his payroll) giving him attitude, challenging his authority, or rebelling against his orders?

Of course not.

And one reason why is, he doesn't place anyone on a pedestal.

Neither does the Joker.

Or Don (or Michael) Corleone

Or Darth Vader (*Star Wars* episodes 4 through 6).

Or Loki.

Or Bane.

Or even Dr. Evil.

Instead, you know what Villains do put on a pedestal?

Their Mission

Their mission — whether it be money, revenge, or conquering the world — always takes priority.

And you must do the same thing if you want the kind of mass charisma and power wielded by the most influential and respected Villains of all time. To paraphrase Dan Kennedy from his

bestselling book *NO BS Time Management*:
The highly charismatic Villain doesn't
need to point a gun at anyone to take
what he wants; people cheerfully <u>give</u> him
what he wants.

And the reason why is, they don't give
anyone their power by pedestalizing
them.

Here's something else to think about:

When you put someone on a pedestal the
only way they can see you is by looking
down on you. And when that happens,
the resulting loss of respect, loyalty,
power, and submission is as predictable
as it is preventable. Historically, many a
man has lost his Villain status, freedom,
dignity, or life by putting a treacherous
dame (Samson in the Bible), corrupt
advisor (King Théoden in *The Lord of the
Rings* books), or even a parent (John
Locke in the TV show *Lost*) on a
pedestal.

For a successful Villain it's just the
opposite.

People in a Villain's life put him on a pedestal — due to his ruthless pursuit of his mission and irresistible charisma — which means they have no choice but to look up to see him.

So never put anything on a pedestal but your mission.

Your mission will never leave you or forsake you. Never nag at you or complain to you. Never betray you or sabotage you. Instead, it'll give you focus. And passion. And purpose. All of which will make you instantly more charismatic, attractive, and influential — someone people are anxious to follow, obey, and submit to.

Bottom line?

Don't mistreat, belittle, or be a dick to anyone.

But don't put them on a pedestal, either.

The only thing you should put on a pedestal is your mission.

That is, if you don't want to suffer the same fate as today's non-Villains who submit to the world, instead of having the world submit to them.

Chapter 6

-

Execute Your Inner Nice Guy with Extreme Prejudice

*"Your compassion is a weakness
your enemies will not share."*

— Henri Ducard
aka, the Villainous Ra's al Ghul

A true story:

A couple years back, I broke one of my own rules when dealing with people in business. What happened was, a non-paying customer sent me a question and I wrote back a detailed email (with advice others have paid me hundreds of dollars for) about what he should do. Then, I (figuratively) swatted him on the ass, wished him luck, and sent him on his merry way thinking he'd be grateful and happy for the free information.

But, it wasn't so.

Like a homeless cat will do if you feed it just one time — he came back looking for MORE free advice, ideas, and time.

Of course, I ignored him.

(That kind of ungrateful low class jackassery is not rewarded.)

Then, a few weeks later I see the guy bad mouthing me in forums, social media, and various groups.

All Because... I Was *Nice*

And it was 100% my own fault.

I should have known better than to let my inner nice guy out of his dungeon that day. (And yes, my inner nice guy has long since been blindfolded, put on his knees, and shot in the head execution-style.)

Listen up, listen good, and never forget, Villain:

Being nice is one of the worst things you can ever do not only to yourself, but to everyone around you. Being nice makes you the exact opposite of a charismatic and influential Villain (it's right up there with being needy)... and does nothing but leave a swath of destruction in its wake every time.

I learned this a long time ago.

(The hard way.)

I was not born a Villain. Frankly, I was the exact opposite of a Villain for most of my life. I was syrupy nice and sweet to everyone. I always put other people before myself. Did favors for people who didn't deserve it. Let people walk all over me. Allowed dames to use me for time, money, and resources (without giving up anything in return). And (worst of all) even gave respect to those who didn't respect me back.

Needless to say, life sucked.

That is, until one day I asked myself:

"What has being 'nice' ever gotten me?"

The answer?

- **Dumped (or friend zoned) by women** — while they pursued the jerks who were not nice.

- **Passed up for promotions** — while the office politicians who savaged morale got big pay raises every quarter.

- **Beaten in business** — as competitors sensed my weakness.

- **Taken advantage of** — spending all my time taking care of everyone else's problems, errands, and requests before mine to show what a "nice guy" I was, even when these same people could have done all these things themselves.

- **Preyed upon** — by scammers, liars, thieves, opportunistic dames, and low life's because I wanted to be "liked."

And the list goes on.

Being nice is not only foolish, it's destructive. And when I changed course and stopped being nice, my entire life changed seemingly overnight. Money, time, dames, opportunity, access, influence, friendship, love... all came flooding in out of nowhere. It was as if I'd been living in a dreary black & white world and was now living in full HD color with surround sound.

What about you?

Are you a nice guy?

Then here's the good news:

It's not too late to change your wicked nice ways. All you have to do is follow my lead on this: Find your inner nice guy, make him get on his knees, and shoot him execution style.

But, to clarify:

This does *not* mean you should start being a dick to people.

Or mistreat anyone.

Or be abusive.

Slaying your inner nice guy means doing things like:

- Laying down boundaries for what is (and is not) acceptable

- Eject low class jackass people out of your life and immediately end toxic relationships (friendships, relationships, business deals, etc)

- Have standards with who you will give your time, attention, love, help, resources, and assistance to

- If you're good at something never do it for free (hat tip to The Joker)

- Be selfish (just like when you're in an airplane, if the cabin loses air pressure, you put your own oxygen mask on before you help anyone else, so it is in every aspect of life)

- Give no quarter to anyone trying to harm you in any way, shape, or form (why nourish and make stronger a rabid dog trying to maul you?)

- Never respect anyone who doesn't respect you back

- Don't put anyone on a pedestal

Bottom line?

Destroy your inner nice guy with extreme prejudice. Then, watch as everything in your life starts to fall into place: Dames treating you differently. Family and friends reacting to you differently. And colleagues, business associates, and bosses responding to you differently (in a good way — with respect instead of pity).

Chapter 7
-
Stake & Behead The Time Vampires

"...They say time is the fire in which we burn. Right now, Captain, my time is running out."

— Tolian Soran
Star Trek Generations

One of the best books I ever read for not only business, but life in general (and should be mandatory for all Villains) is Dan Kennedy's magnificent tome:

NO BS Time Management

Specifically, chapters 4 & 5 (about how having self-discipline and being punctual will almost instantly grant you power over other people) and Chapter 2 — which is about what he calls "Time Vampires."

What are Time Vampires?

They are people who will use, abuse, and take your time (the single most precious commodity a Villain possesses — as time is everything when it comes to executing ideas, planning heists, and having all your Villainous machinations running on all cylinders), and suck every ounce of your natural, Villain-granted charisma and influence out of your body and mind. Dan Kennedy mentions several Time Vampires in the book:

Like Mr. Have-You-Got-A-Minute?

And Mr. Meeting.

And Mr. Trivia.

And so on and so forth.

(As Dan Kennedy says: *"There are almost as many different varieties of Time Vampires as there are birds and butterflies."*)

And you know what?

I can virtually guarantee you... the moment you decide to pursue your Mission, the Time Vampires in your life will awaken in their coffins, rise up, and attempt to turn your neck into a pin cushion.

More:

The Time Vampires skimming the shadows that have an especially voracious appetite for a Villain's time are:

- **The Debating Dracula** — These are friends, family, social media "friends", dames, or insubordinate henchmen & minions who want to debate everything. They like to lurk in the shadowy corners of Facebook, forums, or anywhere else they can hide behind a computer lobbing insults, nay-saying, and passive-aggressive comments at you. Their goal is to suck you into a pissing match "vortex" where you give them all your attention and time, instead of investing that time into your Mission and life. Long, pointless debates nourishes these wicked things... and the more time and attention you give them, the stronger they get, while you merely get weaker.

- **The Phone Calling Count Chokula** — This Time Vampire has an almost "cartoonish" quality to him. He loves to call his Villain friends up and engage in mindless small talk, tell lame jokes, and gossip. He looks innocent and his voice is 100% non-threatening. But, once he gets a toehold into your time on the phone, he will feed and feed and feed... until you're too exhausted to focus on anything else afterwards.

- **The "I'll Be Right Back" Barnabas Collins** — The insidious thing about this Time Vampire is he doesn't even know he IS a Time Vampire. In fact, he is often positioned in your gang somewhere. In many cases, he is instrumental in pulling off heists and implementing your plans. And he is notorious for having information you need, but withholding it for hours and days. For example: You will be in the middle of a conversation with him, he's about to give you the secret vault code... only to tell you something's come up and he'll be back later. Except, he doesn't come back any time soon and your plans go up in smoke.

- **The Always-Late Lestat** — When it comes to Time Vampires, it doesn't get much more annoying (and potentially dangerous) than this cunning time sucker. This Time Vampire thrives off of being late to everything — meetings, appointments, dates (yes, many of these Time Vampires are of the female persuasion), interviews, and the list goes on. Often, they get off on the perceived power being late gives them, thinking it puts them in control. And, let's face it, for many people, it does. When you control someone's time, you control them. Be careful of this one, Villain. This Time Vampire is always thirsty, and will suck every drop of your time away by making you wait for them, wasting your day away, and keeping you from completing your goals in a timely manner.

- **The Nagging Nosferatu** — Every time one of these ugly, mutilated-looking Time Vampires talks to you, you have to be ready to douse it with holy water and drive him (or her) out of your lair into the burning sunlight. They thrive on interrupting Villains — and always at the worst possible time — with an endless barrage of favors, questions, complaints, requests, and brain farts. And the worst part is, if they manage to sink their fangs into you once, they will have a "taste" for you (and ONLY you) so strong, you may not ever be able to fully get rid of them.

- **The Count of Chronic Texting** — This "strain" of Time Vampires are almost always either dames or needy men. When they send you a text (or email) they expect you to drop everything you are doing (no exceptions) and text them back immediately. And if you don't? They will proceed to send you many more texts until you do. Then what happens is, if you start replying right away on a regular basis (and this is particularly true if they know they are interrupting something important) it's like tapping your jugular over and over and over — encouraging them to do more of the same. In some ways, these are the most powerful and deadly (to your Mission) of the Time Vampires.

- **Bride of Debating Dracula** — The Debating Dracula's bride is often a Women's Studies major or just a garden-variety obnoxious feminist. If you find yourself in the same room, vehicle, or group as her... she will draw you into her time-sucking web by airing her unsolicited (and demonstrably false) views on feminism, dating, sexual harassment, politics, religion, etc. Once you take the bait and tell her what an ass she is or try to argue against her emotions, her hook is set and she will reel you in, pounce on you, and rip your throat open, drinking deeply of your time and emotions — leaving little or none of those precious commodities left over for your Mission.

There are more Time Vampire types than this of course. But, the above are the most common ones.

Question now is... what do you do about them?

The answer is simple and twofold:

1. Don't even invite them in! Just like the undead vampires of old, Time Vampires can only attack you if you "invite" them in.

2. If they do get in... ignore them.

There is a lot of power in ignoring people (see the next chapter). And in a Time Vampire's case it is like staking them in the heart, cutting off their head, and stuffing their mouth with garlic.

Even better:

Eject them out of your life completely — socially and/or professionally. Doing that is like burning the staked/beheaded/garlic-stuffed body to ashes so it can never come back.

Bottom line?

Time Vampires *are* real.

If you are a Villain, they are hunting you down right now. And, if you let them, they will drain your time away until there's nothing left but a dried out husk (or, even worse, they may decide to turn YOU into a Time Vampire).

So watch your ass, Villain.

Letting Time Vampires desecrate you will not only destroy accomplishing your Mission, but will sap whatever charisma and influence you have built up, too.

Chapter 8
-
Villains Never Lose Sleep Over the Opinions of Sheep

"An ant has no quarrel with a boot."

— Loki
The Avengers

Let's talk about the great (and notorious) General Douglas MacArthur.

Every Villain should study his life carefully.

Specifically, how he handled and interacted with people, got his way (even when all his superiors and the majority were viciously against him), and how he took an almost glee-like pleasure in making other men (even Presidents, in some cases) submit to his will.

For Example

During one of the more famous battles of the Korean War, General MacArthur wanted to land his troops in the Port of Inchon, which was admittedly dangerous and risky, but would give the Allies a huge tactical advantage if it worked. Of course, the Chiefs and armchair generals all had their say, saying no, they couldn't do it, too risky, won't work, etc. These were the people who President Truman relied on for advice and counsel, and were probably considered the most brilliant wartime strategists in the world — always obeyed without question, hesitation, or pause.

What did General MacArthur do?

Keep pleading his case?

Argue?

Get mad?

None of the above.

What he did was, he <u>patiently</u> listened to all the naysaying and nervous-nellying without uttering a single word. Then at the end, when all the Chiefs finished talking and declared their decision not to land in the Port of Inchon, and they'd have to figure something else out (and their word was "final") General MacArthur took his corn-cob pipe out of his mouth, loudly clanked it into the ashtray, stood up, and said:

> *"Gentlemen, I will be landing in Inchon this September or you will have another commander."*

The result?

They dared not argue with the General, submitted to him, and he won the battle in one of the most spectacular upsets in military history.

Anyway, what's the Villainous lesson of the story?

And, how can it make you more charismatic and influential?

The lesson is this:

General MacArthur ignored the sheep.

He had the confidence (some may say arrogance, but I argue it was justified) to know he was right, acted on it, and wasn't afraid to lose everything (even his career) to go after it (i.e. zero neediness).

There's a saying:

A lion doesn't lose sleep over the opinion of sheep.

And, I'll add, neither do Villains.

What do I mean by "sheep"?

Your henchmen, underlings, sidekicks, dames, employees, friends, bosses, clients, customers, and anyone else who tries to stop, shame, or deter you away from your Mission with their insecure doubts, naysaying, nagging, fear-mongering, or uninformed opinions.

Here's another example:

I recently heard a clip of someone calling into Howard Stern's show offering "constructive criticism." Before the man (who had never created a 9-figure per year talk show empire like Howard has) could rattle off even one of his opinions, Stern interjects:

"Not necessary."

"What's that?"

"Not necessary."

"No... no... but it is, you need feedback because..."

"No I don't. I don't need any feedback. I come in here and I do what I want. What do I need your feedback for?"

Then Stern goes on to tell the guy (who said the show was a "community") that if he thought of the show as a community he'd be doomed and the guy's feedback is irrelevant. Throughout his entire career he didn't ask people their feedback, he doesn't care what any one person thinks, and that's the way he became an innovator — by ignoring the feedback.

In fact, Howard Stern goes on to say about the guy:

"What has he created? If I listen to him and every other asshole I won't have a show. I'll be packed up."

And that, Villain, is the key to being the lion and not the sheep:

Go after your Mission without apology, excuse, or hesitation. If you need guidance, pick your advisors carefully. (i.e. people who have achieved what you are trying to achieve.) And, ignore sheep: the naysayers and unsolicited feedback-givers who try to tell you to do things that are not in line with your goals and strategy.

Yes, they'll get annoyed.

Yes, they'll get "offended."

And, yes, they'll likely get nasty.

But who cares?

What good does it do to fight, argue, or even so much as explain yourself to those who are beneath you?

Does this sound asshole-ish?

Good.

A great teacher is often not nice, accommodating, or seeeeeensitive to anyone's feelings. Frankly, you are doing them a favor in as much as psychologists have proven that ignoring someone causes the same reaction in their brain as physical pain. And what better teacher is there than pain?

Anyway, to wrap up:

Ignore the sheep.

Let them graze and baaaaaa! on someone else's lawn. And, if they come walking onto your lawn, turn them into lamb stew by ignoring them, doing things your way, and letting them know (via your actions and success, without having to say a word), you don't care what they think, say, or do. The result will be ratcheting up your charisma and influence by dozens of notches.

Chapter 9

-

Patience: A Super Villain's Deadliest Weapon

*"I have experience and patience.
A man can do anything if he has those"*

— Zemo
Captain America 3: Civil War

One movie every Villain should not only watch but memorize, is the 2002 version of *The Count of Monte Cristo. (WARNING: Before reading further, watch the movie if you haven't seen it already.* Spoilers galore...)

Here's why you should study it:

The movie is about a young man (Edmond Dantes) recently promoted to ship captain and about to marry his woman, who is then betrayed by his best friend, co-worker, and a corrupt official, and falsely imprisoned, with his loved ones thinking him dead. The prison is a hell hole — a small room, with nobody else to talk to and nothing to sit or sleep on. He gets a small bowl of slop to eat (with his fingers) each night, and there's nothing to do except sit and count the stones in his cell. The only "escape" is death by suicide or natural causes.

But that's not even the worst part.

The deranged warden admits to Edmond he's innocent, and he shouldn't be there, because the prison (called the *Chateau D'iff*) is where the government sends the prisoners they're "ashamed" of. And just to remind the prisoners (even though they're innocent) how long they've been there, the warden whips them each year on their anniversary.

For five years Edmond rots in this prison.

Nothing to do.

Nobody to talk to.

Not a smidgen of a hope for escape.

Until one evening he hears movement under the stone floor. At first, Edmond is freaked out — thinking it's a monster coming to get him.

But it's not a monster.

It's a man.

Specifically, an old Priest who used to be a solider in Napoleon's army for withholding information on where a vast treasure is hidden. And in exchange for Edmond's help digging, the Priest agrees to educate him on reading, writing, science, economics, and fighting.

Long story short:

After 8 more years Edmond escapes. But, not before the Priest (with his dying breath) tells him where that treasure he was imprisoned for not telling about is hidden. A treasure, Edmond decides, he will use to get his revenge.

And get his revenge he does...

One by one, Edmond's enemies fall into his traps as he outwits, outthinks, and out maneuvers the people who betrayed him 13 years earlier.

What is the point of telling you about this?

Because this movie shows how someone can go from complete despair and ruin — betrayed and falsely imprisoned for over 13 years — to becoming the "proverbial" charismatic and influential Villain. Frankly, there's nothing about Edmond that's not charismatic.

For example, he's:

- Wealthy.

- Loyal to his true friends.

- Lethal to his enemies (taking them down one-by-one without dirtying his own hands in most cases).

- A badass fighter — by sword, knife, and hand-to-hand.

- Stylishly dressed.

- In control of his emotions.

- Able to harness his negative feelings to achieve his goals.

- Capable of keeping his wits (even when in mortal danger).

- Immune to the charms of women.

- Saddled with a cool title (when you're called "Count" people can't help but find you charismatic and influential)

- Not "nice" (admitting, "I'm a Count, not a saint.")

And the list goes on... including the one all-important trait (that is mandatory if you want to be a charismatic and influential Villain) that made his escape and revenge possible.

And that trait is: **Patience**.

Edmond never would have escaped without patience. And, he couldn't have so perfectly plotted his enemies' downfalls one-by-one, setting each trap with inhuman precision, with every variable controlled and action predicted in advance, without patience. Patience is a

Villain's deadliest weapon. Patience is 100 times rarer than gold and 1000 times more valuable. A Villain with patience is not just a villain — but a *Super Villain*. As one of my favorite "real life" Villains A.B. Dada said:

> *"When asked what is the sexiest part of a man, my answer has never wavered: Patience. Patience is erotic, impatience is childish. A man who can wait to make a decision until it's best for him is a man a woman can trust to lead. A man who hurries things is a man who is uncertain about his future options: he wants to spend his little power now in case he loses the chance. Not looks, not height, not fitness, not intelligence, not wealth, not clothes, not humor. Patience."*

And make no mistake, Villain:

This goes beyond picking up dames. Patience seeps into every aspect of your life — professional, personal, family, friendships, achieving your Mission, and more. That's why, whatever patience you have you must always nurture it.

Grow it.

Strengthen it.

And, yes, *patiently* take care of it.

Be conscious of your patience, and exercise it like a muscle at every opportunity. By becoming the most patient man you know, you will move mountains while leaving all your enemies, competitors, haters, and nay-sayers in the dust — mouths gaping, wondering how you beat them.

Chapter 10
-
Be the Joker

"It's not about money, it's about sending a message. Everything burns!"

— The Joker
The Dark Knight

I want to end this book on how to be a charismatic and influential Villain by examining one of the greatest Villains of all time:

The Joker.

But first, some context...

I'm not saying to be a psychopath. Or bleach your skin. Or kill mass quantities of people for kicks. But, there is something that makes the Joker perhaps the most well-known (and most feared — by both heroes and other Villains alike) Villain in the world. An "attribute" that, if you apply it to your everyday life, will not only make your bad self a more charismatic and influential Villain... but also put more dough in your bank account, attract more dames into your life, and keep your enemies constantly on the defense, fearing your next move, and always struggling to keep up with you.

What attribute do I speak of?

Impact

A Villain who understands the power of having impact in every word he says, every story he tells, and every move he makes, is a Villain who never has to worry about money, broads, success, access, opportunity, fame, or anything else he desires.

What do I mean by "impact", exactly?

Well, let's analyze how The Joker does it.

If any Villain has mastered the ability to have indifference-crushing impact, it's him. No matter what incarnation of the Joker you study (movies, animated shows, comic books, etc) the one thing The Joker has the ability to do more than anyone else (including Batman) is making everything he does unforgettably impactful.

Love him, hate him, or leave him — you never forget The Joker or anything he says or does.

He never bores you.

There is no indifference.

(Indifference is a Villain's arch enemy in many ways.)

And, everything he says or does sticks in your mind.

This kind of impact creates fear in his enemies (and even in his fellow Villains), loyalty in his henchmen (and especially his dame), and makes him supremely charismatic and influential (even to those who are scared, repulsed, or amused by him).

Here are just a few examples of how The Joker has impact:

- Tells unforgettable stories ("Want to know how I got these scars...?")

- **Unpredictable** (which is the exact opposite of boring — boredom is like kryptonite to a Villain)

- **Funny** (he ain't called The "Joker" for nothin')

- **Turns his enemies' plans around on them** (like a puppet master, he controls his enemies' actions, who are ultimately always reacting to him, with them completely unaware of it until it's too late)

- **Changes the rules on a dime** (constantly keeping his enemies and the cops dancing to his beat, never giving them a chance to go on offense)

- **Peacocking** (his chalk-white skin, blood-red lips, and clown-green hair makes him always stands out in a room, in a crowd, or even in an asylum, creating instant impact)

- **Escalates** (his plans and machinations are always becoming more complex, more deadly, and, yes, more impactful)

- **Keeps expanding his ambitions** (he might start off by ripping off mob bosses, but then gets bored and seeks a new Mission — like killing Batman, or taking over the mob, for example)

- **Not affected by money** (even though he's a master criminal and thief, he'd just as soon burn a pile of money than spend it, this contrast is extremely impactful to his enemies)

- **Thinks deeper than anyone else** (he's able to control his enemies simply by thinking 50 steps ahead while they only think 2 or 3 steps ahead)

- **Pursues excellence** (he's disgusted by the current flock of criminals, knows HIS city deserves better, and then does something about it)

- **No fear** (he fears nothing — not incarceration, not an ass beating, and not death, even going so far as willingly letting Two-Face put a gun to his forehead and flip a coin to decide to kill him or not)

- **Dangerous** (even though The Joker has no super powers he is perhaps the most dangerous Villain on the planet — and everyone knows it)

Fact is, people are attracted to these traits because they give a Villain impact. And a Villain who knows how to create impact is a Villain who people can't help but want to follow and submit to. It doesn't matter what you look like, how deep your voice is, how ugly you are, how short you are, how bald you are, or how humble your beginnings are. If the ability to create impact can make even a skinny, creepy, and goofy-looking guy like The Joker charismatic and influential... imagine what they can do to a Villain like you (with little or none of his defects) on a Mission?

Moral of the story?

Whatever you do, always do it with *impact*.

Only then, a true Villain will you be.

To sum up this book it's only fitting to paraphrase the Joker's famous quote:

> *"This world needs a better class of Villain. And we're going to give it to them."*

I hope you enjoyed this book on how to become more charismatic and influential. And, even more important, I hope it's made you a more persuasive man, a better person, and, yes, a more powerful Villain.

For an ongoing "Villainous" education in email marketing, copywriting, selling, and persuasion, go here next:

www.BenSettle.com

Dastardly Disclosures
& Disclaimers

This book is published in electronic file formats for e-reader devices and software. Neither the Author nor the Publisher makes any claim to the intellectual property rights of publishers, their subsidiaries, or related entities.

All trademarks and service marks are the properties of their respective owners. All references to these properties are made solely for editorial purposes. Except for marks actually owned by the Author or the Publisher, no commercial claims are made to their use, and neither the Author nor the Publisher is affiliated with such marks in any way.

Unless otherwise expressly noted, none of the individuals or business entities mentioned herein has endorsed the contents of this book.

Limits of Liability & Disclaimers of Warranties

Because this book is a general educational information product, it is not a substitute for professional advice on the topics discussed in it.

The materials in this book are provided "as is" and without warranties of any kind either express or implied. The Author and the Publisher disclaim all warranties, express or implied, including, but not limited to, implied warranties of merchantability and fitness for a particular purpose. The Author and the Publisher do not warrant that defects will be corrected, or that any website or any server that makes this book available is free of viruses or other harmful components. The Author does not warrant or make any representations regarding the use or the results of the use of the materials in this book in terms of their correctness, accuracy, reliability, or otherwise. Applicable law may not allow the exclusion of implied warranties, so the above exclusion may not apply to you.

Under no circumstances, including, but not limited to, negligence, shall the Author or the Publisher be liable for any special or consequential damages that result from the use of, or the inability to use this book, even if the Author, the Publisher, or an authorized representative has been advised of the possibility of such damages. Applicable law may not allow the limitation or exclusion of liability or incidental or consequential damages, so the above limitation or exclusion may not apply to you. In no event shall the Author or Publisher total liability to you for all damages, losses, and causes of action (whether in contract, tort, including but not limited to, negligence or otherwise) exceed the amount paid by you, if any, for this book.

You agree to hold the Author and the Publisher of this book, principals, agents, affiliates, and employees harmless from any and all liability for all claims for damages due to injuries, including attorney fees and costs, incurred by you or caused to third parties by you, arising out of the products, services, and activities discussed in this book, excepting only claims for gross negligence or intentional tort.

You agree that any and all claims for gross negligence or intentional tort shall be settled solely by confidential binding arbitration per the American Arbitration Association's commercial arbitration rules. All arbitration must occur in the municipality where the Author's principal place of business is located. Arbitration fees and costs shall be split equally, and you are solely responsible for your own lawyer fees.

Facts and information are believed to be accurate at the time they were placed in this book. All data provided in this book is to be used for information purposes only. The information contained within is not intended to provide specific legal, financial, tax, physical or mental health advice, or any other advice whatsoever, for any individual or company and should not be relied upon in that regard. The services described are only offered in jurisdictions where they may be legally offered. Information provided is not all-inclusive, and is limited to information that is made available and such information should not be relied upon as all-inclusive or accurate.

For more information about this policy, please contact the Author at the e-mail address listed in the Copyright Notice at the front of this book.

IF YOU DO NOT AGREE WITH THESE TERMS AND EXPRESS CONDITIONS, DO NOT READ THIS BOOK. YOUR USE OF THIS BOOK, PRODUCTS, SERVICES, AND ANY PARTICIPATION IN ACTIVITIES MENTIONED IN THIS BOOK, MEAN THAT YOU ARE AGREEING TO BE LEGALLY BOUND BY THESE TERMS.

Affiliate Compensation & Material Connections Disclosure

This book may contain hyperlinks to websites and information created and maintained by other individuals and organizations. The Author and the Publisher do not control or guarantee the accuracy, completeness, relevance, or timeliness of any information or privacy policies posted on these linked websites.

You should assume that all references to products and services in this book are made because material connections exist between the Author or Publisher and the providers of the mentioned products and services ("Provider"). You should also assume that all hyperlinks within this book are affiliate links for (a) the Author, (b) the Publisher, or (c) someone else who is an affiliate for the mentioned products and services (individually and collectively, the "Affiliate").

The Affiliate recommends products and services in this book based in part on a good faith belief that the purchase of such products or services will help readers in general.

The Affiliate has this good faith belief because (a) the Affiliate has tried the product or service mentioned prior to recommending it or (b) the Affiliate has researched the reputation of the Provider and has made the decision to recommend the Provider's products or services based on the Provider's history of providing these or other products or services.

The representations made by the Affiliate about products and services reflect the Affiliate's honest opinion based upon the facts known to the Affiliate at the time this book was published.

Because there is a material connection between the Affiliate and Providers of products or services mentioned in this book, you should always assume that the Affiliate may be biased because of the Affiliate's relationship with a Provider and/or because the Affiliate has received or will receive something of value from a Provider.

Perform your own due diligence before purchasing a product or service mentioned in this book.

The type of compensation received by the Affiliate may vary. In some instances, the Affiliate may receive complimentary products (such as a review copy), services, or money from a Provider prior to mentioning the Provider's products or services in this book.

In addition, the Affiliate may receive a monetary commission or non-monetary compensation when you take action by clicking on a hyperlink in this book. This includes, but is not limited to, when you purchase a product or service from a Provider after clicking on an affiliate link in this book.

Purchase Price

Although the Publisher believes the price is fair for the value that you receive, you understand and agree that the purchase price for this book has been arbitrarily set by the Publisher. This price bears no relationship to objective standards.

Due Diligence

You are advised to do your own due diligence when it comes to making any decisions. Use caution and seek the advice of qualified professionals before acting upon the contents of this book or any other information. You shall not consider any examples, documents, or other content in this book or otherwise provided by the Author or Publisher to be the equivalent of professional advice.

The Author and the Publisher assume no responsibility for any losses or damages resulting from your use of any link, information, or opportunity contained in this book or within any other information disclosed by the Author or the Publisher in any form whatsoever.

YOU SHOULD ALWAYS CONDUCT YOUR OWN INVESTIGATION

(PERFORM DUE DILIGENCE) BEFORE BUYING PRODUCTS OR SERVICES FROM ANYONE OFFLINE OR VIA THE INTERNET. THIS INCLUDES PRODUCTS AND SERVICES SOLD VIA HYPERLINKS EMBEDDED IN THIS BOOK.

Made in the USA
Coppell, TX
16 March 2020

16963815R00066